Arctic Wildlife

3rd Edition

Includes:

Arctic Biomes

Habitats and Habits

Bird Activities

Mammal Activities

Reptile & Amphibian Activities

Invertebrate Activities

Wildlife Respect

Waterford Press

www.waterfordpress.com

Introduction

The Arctic region includes three major biomes – the tundra, the taiga (boreal forest) and the Arctic Ocean. A biome is a large region that has similar plants, animals and organisms that have adapted to the geography and climate of that area. A biome can have several ecosystems.

An ecosystem is a community of organisms that interact with one another and with their environment. Several ecosystems can exist within a biome.

Ecosystems within the three major biomes of the Arctic include rivers, lakes, streams, ponds, wetlands, mountains, forests, coastal cliffs and marine ecosystems such as ocean shelves and sea ice.

A diverse range of animals live in the Arctic, including grizzlies, wolves, caribou, musk oxen, whales, seals, and many species of fish, birds and crustaceans, including crabs, lobsters and krill.

Arctic Biomes

Tundra Biome

The tundra is a cold, treeless landscape that covers about 20% of the Earth's land surface. It is the coldest biome, with an average temperature of -18°F (-27°C), but it gets even colder in the winter. Summers are very short. The ground below the top soil is frozen year round, and snow covers the ground nine months of the year, making it difficult for plants to grow. Because of the harsh conditions, very few animals live in the tundra all year long. Many, like caribou and the American golden plover, move to warmer areas to find food when snow arrives. There are two types of tundra: alpine and arctic. Alpine tundra is high in the mountains above the tree line. The Arctic tundra is in the far north along the Arctic Circle.

Taiga Forest Biome

The taiga is the driest and coldest forest biome. It is sometimes called the boreal forest or the coniferous forest because it is covered with coniferous (evergreen) trees. The taiga is the largest land biome. Winter lasts about six months, with temperatures as low as -65°F (-54°C). Summers are warmer but very short. Taiga forests are found in the far north between the temperate forest biome (forests with a moderate climate) and the tundra biome. Russia and Siberia have the largest taiga forests, but this biome is also found in Canada and the United States (Alaska) and Scandinavia (Finland, Norway and Sweden). Some animals that live in the taiga include reindeer, wolverine and the boreal chorus frog.

Ocean Biome (Arctic Ocean)

The Arctic Ocean is the smallest ocean on Earth. It is located in the farthest north part of the planet. The North Pole is near its center. Several islands exist on the edges of the ocean, but there are none in the center, which has a permanent cover of ice. The Arctic Ocean has two types of ice: sea ice and pack ice. Seawater that freezes and melts depending on the season is called sea ice. When a mass of sea ice remains frozen year after year, it is called pack ice. Sea ice is saltier and less smooth than pack ice. The ecosystems of the Arctic Ocean are home to several large predators such as walruses, whales and polar bears.

Class Act

Animals can be sorted into categories based on certain characteristics. The system for sorting animals into categories is called taxonomy. Mammals, birds, fish, reptiles and amphibians belong to a class of animals called vertebrates. Vertebrates are animals with backbones. Invertebrates are another class of animals that do not have backbones (like insects, worms and spiders).

Draw a line between the Arctic animal and its class.

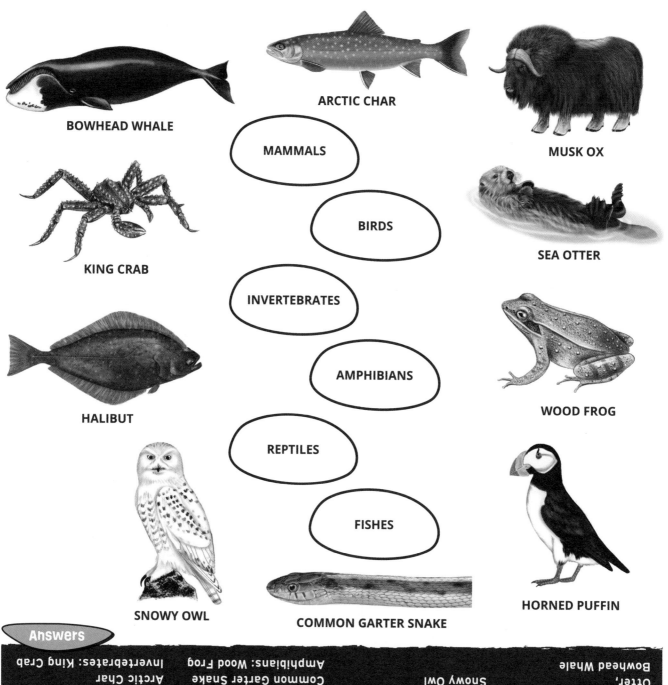

BOWHEAD WHALE

ARCTIC CHAR

MUSK OX

MAMMALS

KING CRAB

BIRDS

SEA OTTER

INVERTEBRATES

HALIBUT

AMPHIBIANS

WOOD FROG

REPTILES

SNOWY OWL

FISHES

COMMON GARTER SNAKE

HORNED PUFFIN

You Are What You Eat

Herbivores eat mostly plants. Carnivores eat other animals.
Omnivores eat plants and animals.

Draw a line between the Arctic animal and its diet.

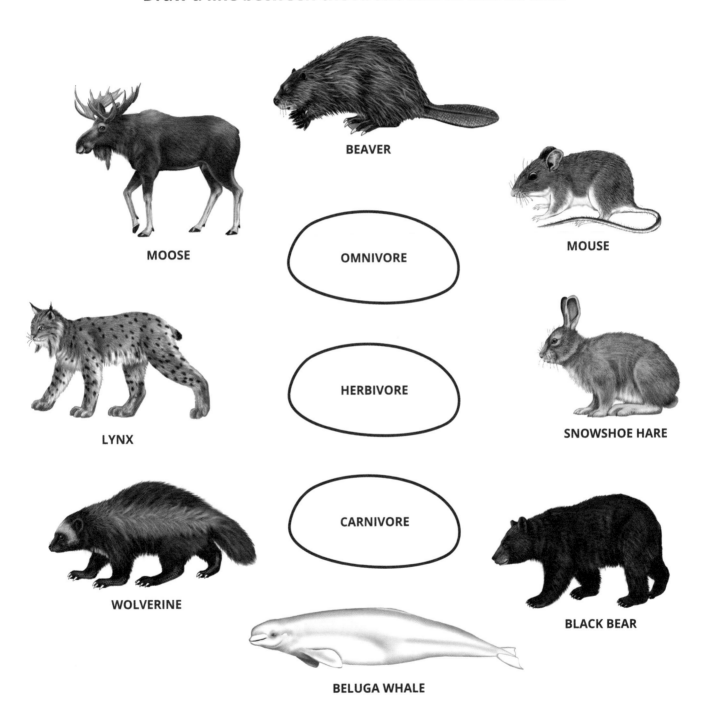

MOOSE

BEAVER

MOUSE

OMNIVORE

LYNX

HERBIVORE

SNOWSHOE HARE

WOLVERINE

CARNIVORE

BLACK BEAR

BELUGA WHALE

Food Chain

A food chain is the order in which animals feed on other plants and animals. All living things need each other. For instance, a simple food chain might be: seeds to deer mouse to snowy owl.

Producers – A producer takes the sun's energy and stores it as food.

Consumers – A consumer feeds on other living things to get energy. Consumers can include herbivores, carnivores and omnivores.

Decomposers – A decomposer consumes waste and dead organisms for energy.

Label each living organism below as a producer, consumer or decomposer.

SPRUCE _____

EIDER _____

CARIBOU _____

SNAIL _____

POLAR BEAR _____

ARCTIC WILLOW _____

MINK _____

SHRIMP _____

Home Sweet Home

There are a number of habitats in the Arctic that support a unique community of animals that feed and live there.

Draw a line between the animal and its habitat.
(Note: Many animals can live in several habitats.)

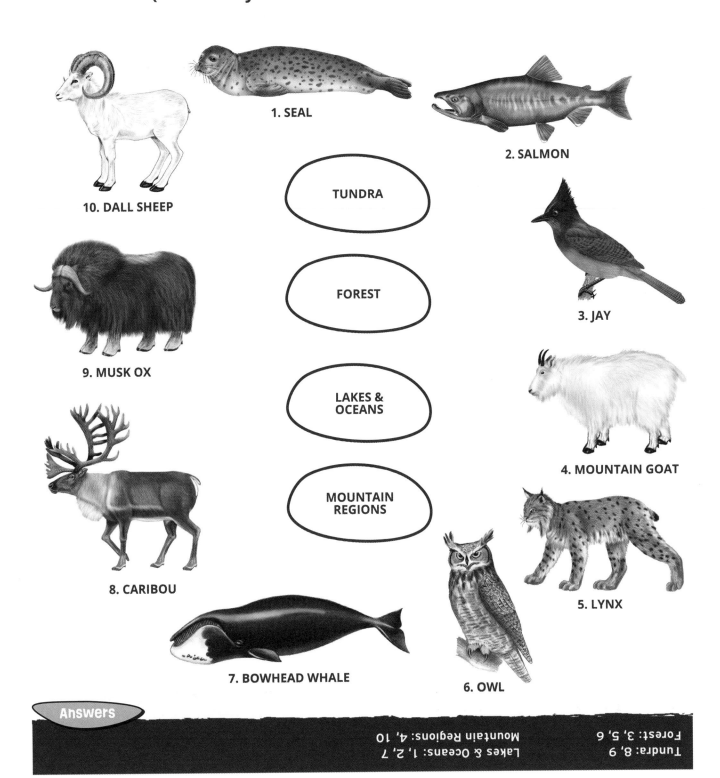

10. DALL SHEEP

1. SEAL

2. SALMON

TUNDRA

FOREST

LAKES & OCEANS

MOUNTAIN REGIONS

9. MUSK OX

3. JAY

4. MOUNTAIN GOAT

8. CARIBOU

5. LYNX

7. BOWHEAD WHALE

6. OWL

Make Words

The **Arctic grayling**
is a colorful Arctic fish with a
distinctive sail-like dorsal fin.
Related to salmon and trout, it lives
in large lakes and rivers and returns
to shallow rocky streams to breed.
It feeds primarily on crustaceans
and insects and is a highly prized
sport fish.

How many words can you make from the letters in its name?

_____   _____

_____   _____

_____   _____

_____   _____

_____   _____

_____   _____

_____   _____

_____   _____

Picture Scramble

Place the numbers 1 through 9 in the lettered boxes on the right to create the images of Arctic animals on the left.

WALRUS

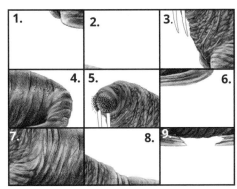
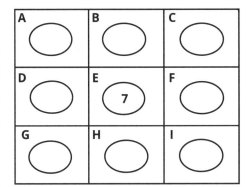

A | B | C
D | E 7 | F
G | H | I

ARCTIC FOX

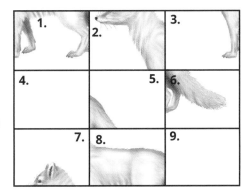
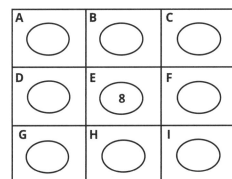

A | B | C
D | E 8 | F
G | H | I

KING CRAB

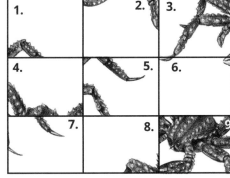
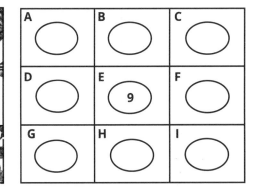

A | B | C
D | E 9 | F
G | H | I

Be An Artist

Draw this puffin by copying it one square at a time.

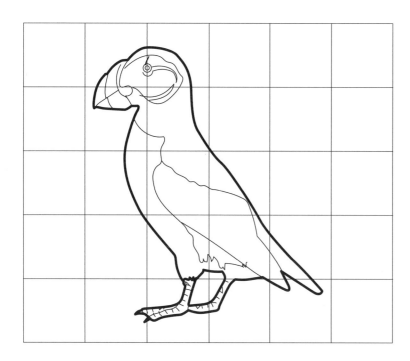

Puffins are stocky, short-winged birds that breed in huge colonies on offshore islands. They feed by diving into the ocean and "flying" underwater in search of small fishes. They have the unique ability to hold up to a dozen small fishes in their beak at one time.

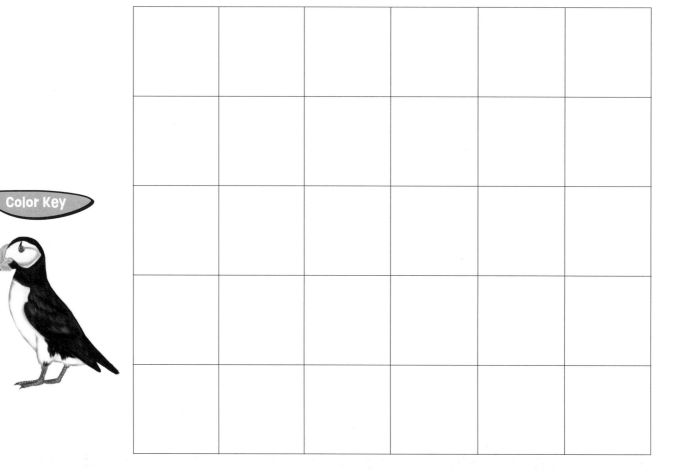

Color Key

Word Search

Find the names of these Arctic mammals.

FLYING SQUIRREL

WOLVERINE

```
F G M T L I D Y G S L C S V P V
N M T B P B Z N A M F L V B D J
O F Q N P V F H L O B A A F Z K
L C E G K Z L T H E M T P Q D F
E M O U S E Y N O E Q I T E I B
M T F Y B R I V E R O T T E R F
M I B W J J N Y R H S I X J C T
I P G P U T G Z F H T V M P H N
N U I W M R S S W Z M B L W P I
G S X O G T Q X M E Z A E B R T
K A Q B P M U C O V A Q R N J W
W O L V E R I N E Y G S Q M V S
H F B N G G R N I K B T E F O U
D O D G C Q R H K H X S Y L T T
K R W C I T E K O S F H E L L W
Y K M B Z D L P I A Z D L T Q U
```

RIVER OTTER

MARMOT

MINK

MOUSE

WEASEL

LEMMING

Answers

11

Name Scramble

Unscramble the letters to form the names of these animals.

1.

F	N	F	I	P	U

2.

A	O	B	C	R	I	U

3.

A	T	B	I	U	L	H

4.

E	A	W	L	H

5.

L	W	O	Y	S	N	W	O

6.

V	N	R	A	E

7.

T	S	O	R	T	E	A	E

8.

R	P	R	L	B	A	O	E	A

Answers

1. Puffin   2. Caribou   3. Halibut   4. Whale   5. Snowy Owl   6. Raven   7. Sea Otter   8. Polar Bear

12

Maze

Sea lions are large marine mammals that feed primarily on fish. Unlike smaller seals, they have the ability to stand up on their front flippers. They are highly social animals and often gather in large groups called rafts. When they are not hunting for fish or taking a dip in the ocean, they can often be spotted sunbathing on rocky beaches and outcroppings.

Help this sea lion find something to eat.

ENTER

Color Me

There are about 2,000 species of **sea star**, all of which live in saltwater. They use tiny tube feet on the underside of their "arms" to move. Their bony, calcified skin protects them from most predators, and many have bright, striking colors – like blue, red or orange – that scare off would-be attackers. These amazing creatures also have the ability to grow new body parts if needed!

Use the Color Key to help you color the picture of the sea star.

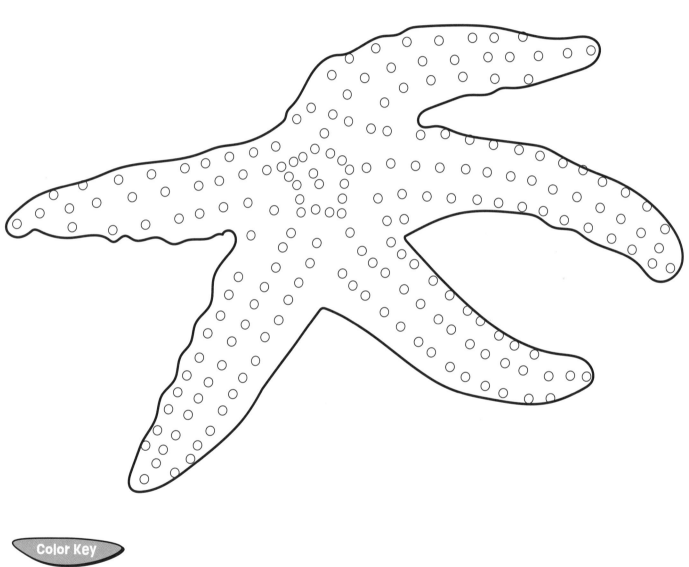

Color Key

Maze

The **Arctic fox** is found throughout the Arctic region. Active throughout the year, its coat is white in winter and brown to bluish-gray in summer. It feeds primarily on small rodents and also steals scraps from the kills of larger mammals like bears and wolves.

Help the Arctic fox find the way to its den.

ENTER

Animal Tracks

Studying tracks is an easy way to discover the kinds of mammals found in an area.

Draw a line between the Arctic mammal and its tracks.

MOUSE

I have light tracks with four toes on my front feet and five toes on my back feet.

BEAVER

My tracks are unique because in soft mud you can see the webbing between my toes.

WOLF

I have tracks like a pet dog, with four toes on each foot. My claws always show.

1.

2.

3.

4.

5.

6.

LYNX

My tracks have rounded toes. My claws don't show because they are retracted when I walk.

CARIBOU

Like most hoofed animals, my tracks have two long toes that make up my track.

SNOWSHOE HARE

I have long back feet and short front feet.

Color Me

Use the Color Key to help you color the pictures below.

The **red fox** is most common south of the Arctic tundra.
It also lives in tundra regions, along with the Arctic fox.

Color Key

The **Lapland longspur** lives in the high Arctic during the summer
and will sing at all hours but mostly in the morning.

Color Key

Name Match

Draw a line between the animal and its name.

1.

2.

3.

4.

5.

6.

7.

8.

TUNDRA SWAN

GREAT BLUE HERON

LION'S MANE JELLYFISH

BLACK-CAPPED CHICKADEE

RED SQUIRREL

CANADA JAY

YELLOW WARBLER

BOREAL TOAD

Word Search

Find the names of these Arctic fishes.

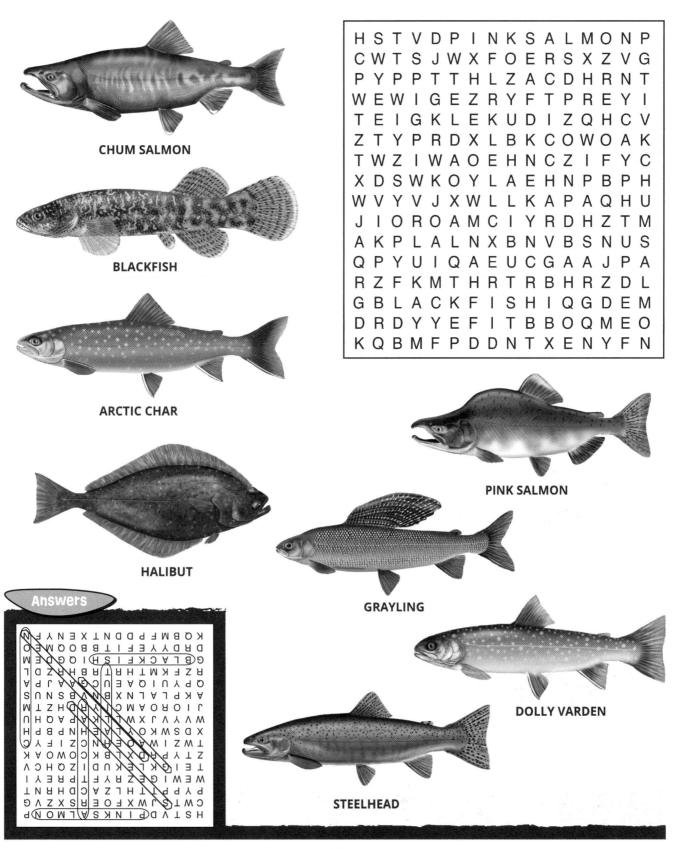

CHUM SALMON

BLACKFISH

ARCTIC CHAR

HALIBUT

PINK SALMON

GRAYLING

DOLLY VARDEN

STEELHEAD

H S T V D P I N K S A L M O N P
C W T S J W X F O E R S X Z V G
P Y P P T T H L Z A C D H R N T
W E W I G E Z R Y F T P R E Y I
T E I G K L E K U D I Z Q H C V
Z T Y P R D X L B K C O W O A K
T W Z I W A O E H N C Z I F Y C
X D S W K O Y L A E H N P B P H
W V Y V J X W L L K A P A Q H U
J I O R O A M C I Y R D H Z T M
A K P L A L N X B N V B S N U S
Q P Y U I Q A E U C G A A J P A
R Z F K M T H R T R B H R Z D L
G B L A C K F I S H I Q G D E M
D R D Y Y E F I T B B O Q M E O
K Q B M F P D D N T X E N Y F N

Answers

19

Name Match

Draw a line between the mammal and its name.

1.

GRIZZLY

WOLVERINE

5.

CARIBOU

2.

MUSK OX

6.

MOOSE

3.

MOUNTAIN GOAT

7.

WOLF

4.

LYNX

8.

20

Be An Artist

Draw this spotted ptarmigan by copying it one square at a time.

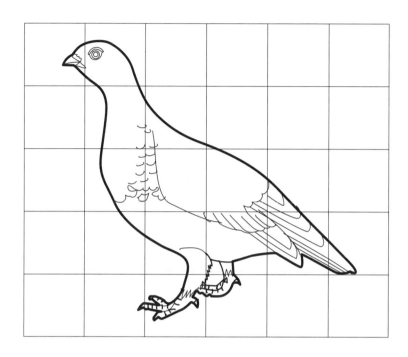

Ptarmigan are chicken-like birds that live in forests and on the tundra. Their plumage is mottled brown in summer and turns all-white in winter to help them hide from predators. They are very protective of their young and will attack intruders to distract them from the nest, including humans and even grizzly bears!

Color Key

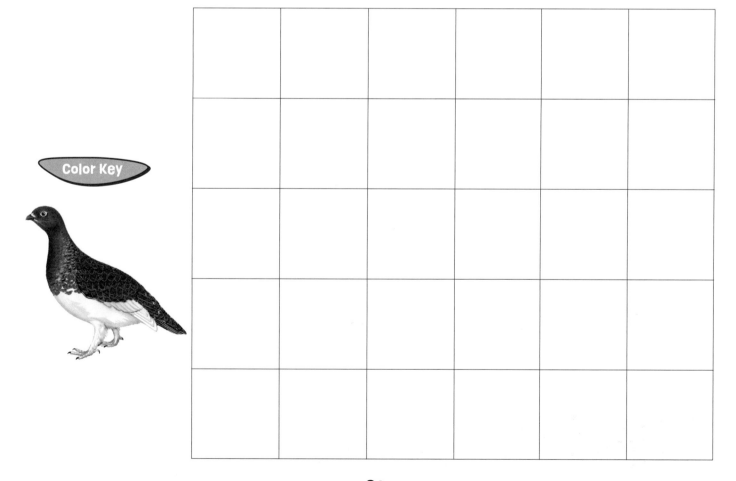

Shadow Know-How

Can you identify these Arctic marine mammals?

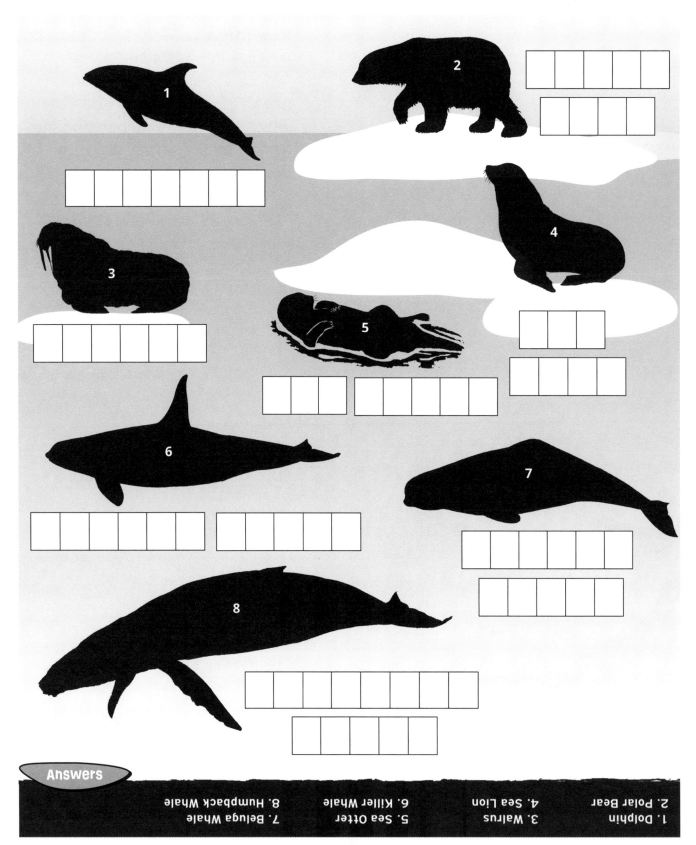

Crossword

Finish these phrases to name some familiar Arctic mammals.

Across

1. White whale.

....

2. Color-changing bunny has big feet.

....

3. Chatterer often scolds people from trees.

....

4. Also known as "devil bear."

....

5. Also known as orca.

....

6. Long-haired cow-like animal has funny-looking horns.

....

Down

7. Hundreds of thousands migrate in herds each year.

....

8. _ _ _ _ _ _ _ bear.

9. Named for large overhanging snout.

....

10. Rhymes with noose.

....

11. Wild dogs hunt in packs.

....

12. Arctic _ _ _ _ _ _ _ _.

Word Search

Find the names of these Arctic birds.

EIDER

```
R O T T P X P T E O J Q Y E G F
C O G R A Z Z T B I U S Z U S H
M Z K N L P U W A L S E K Y Z C
M Y G V F X N J L R Z U L L Q Z
Q L R G M C P Z D N M R L W B P
J Z J T R L T A E I G I W B Y S
C L L B U O U A A D O L G W B Y
P O M B R N S V G V S Y X A I Q
E L Z M D G D B L W H D J F N Z
Q B O J D S G R E U A H E E U U
C Y O V A P L I A A W Q I U R J
X T I E E U D J F S K N D E W D
C F Y H B R F P Z Q W G E E A J
K T N W L I A K V R K A R I N S
V H Q R Y S N B Z P J N N O B D
M U S Y N P B R H A K B W F L S
```

GOSHAWK

BALD EAGLE

LONGSPUR

GROSBEAK

Answers

```
S L F W B K A H R B P N Y S U M
D B O N N J P Z B N S Y R Q H V
S N I R A K R V K A I L W N T K
J A E E G W Q Z P F R B H Y F C
D W E D N K S F D U E E I T X
J R U I Q W A A I L P A V O Y C
U U E E H A U E R G S D J O B Q
Z N F J D H W L B D G D M Z L E
Q I A X Y S V G V S N R B M O P
Y B W G L O D A A U O U B L L C
S Y B W I G I E A T L R T J Z J
P B W L R M N D Z P C M G R L Q
Z Q L L U Z R L J N X F V G Y M
C Z Y K E S L A W U P L N K Z M
H S U Z S U I B T Z Z A R G O C
F G E Y Q J O E T P X P T T O R
```

PLOVER

PTARMIGAN

TUNDRA SWAN

24

Make Words

The **polar bear** is the world's largest carnivore. It spends many months each year on floating sea ice and is considered by many to be a marine mammal like whales and seals. It feeds primarily on seals but has been known to hunt larger prey like walruses and beluga whales.

How many words can you make from the letters in its name?

_____   _____

_____   _____

_____   _____

_____   _____

_____   _____

_____   _____

_____   _____

Answers

Possible answers include: bee, belt, best, bet, bid, bide, bile, bite, bled, blest, blew, debt, delete, dell, dew, eldest, led, list, seed, set, sleet, tweed, web, wed, weed, weld, welt, west, wet, wide, widest, wild, wildest, wile, wiles, wilt

25

Connect The Dots

Polar bears are champion swimmers. They use their large paws to paddle through water while their hind legs act as a rudder.

Follow the numbers to connect the dots and draw this Arctic mammal.

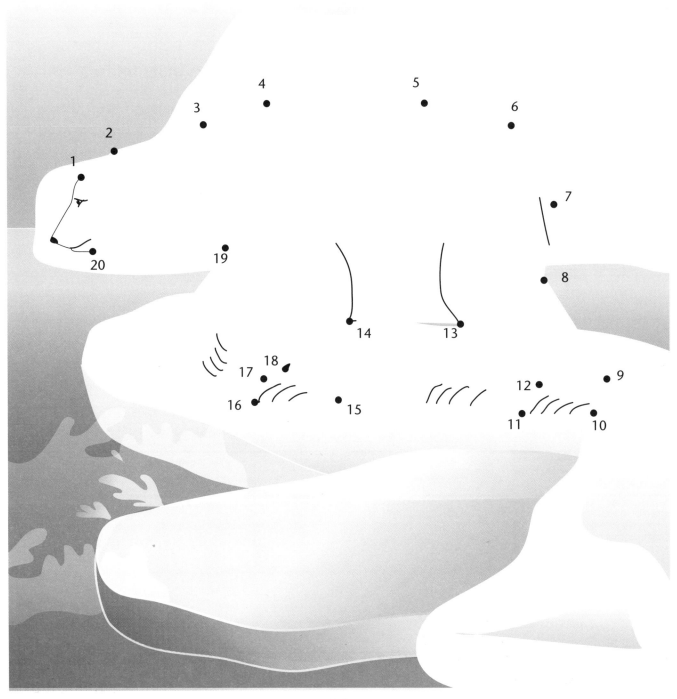

Be an Artist

Draw this Arctic char by copying it one square at a time.
Color your image, using the color key to guide you.

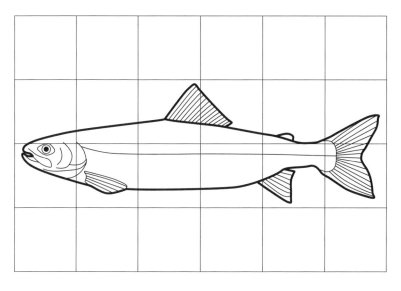

Arctic char is a cold water fish that breeds in freshwater but can be anadromous, which means it may spend parts of its life cycle in both fresh and salt waters. It is found farther north than any other freshwater fish. Its color depends on where it lives and the time of year. It is usually brown or olive green on its upper body and lighter colored with spots on its lower body. Its belly and fins become bright red or orange at spawning.

Color Key

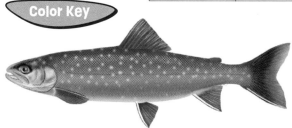

Color Me

One of the most ornately adorned waterfowl in the world, the male **king eider** attempts to impress females by jutting its head forward and swimming around them. In contrast, females have less showy brown and black feathers and a black bill. King eiders nest in the Arctic tundra and migrate south for winter, returning to their breeding areas in spring.

Use the Color Key to help you color the picture of the male king eider.

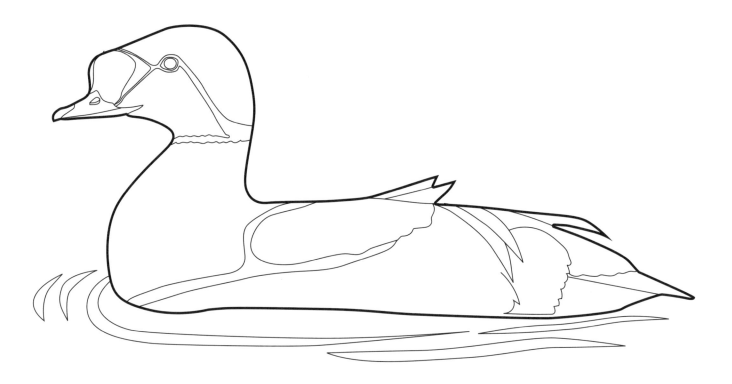

Color Key

Picture Scramble

Place the numbers 1 through 9 in the lettered boxes
on the right to create the image on the left.

RIVER OTTER

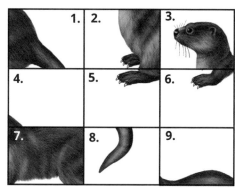

1.	2.	3.
4.	5.	6.
7.	8.	9.

A	B	C
D	E **7**	F
G	H	I

SNOWY OWL

1.	2.	3.
4.	5.	6.
7.	8.	9.

A	B	C
D	E **1**	F
G	H	I

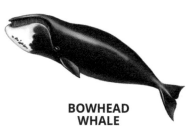

BOWHEAD WHALE

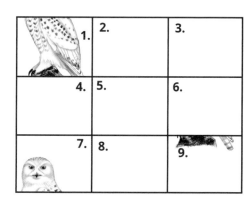
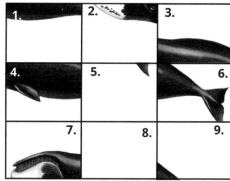

1.	2.	3.
4.	5.	6.
7.	8.	9.

A	B	C
D	E **4**	F
G	H	I

Word Search

Find the names of these Arctic predators.

POLAR BEAR

FALCON

SNOWY OWL

WOLF

LYNX

SEA LION

WOLVERINE

KILLER WHALE

Answers

```
J W H M B H X E W O L F L X U W
F Q P R W L Z X B X N A Q H R M
K A C Z O W P B A H C L K P C Q
N C T B Z P O U D H H C R W U W
W V H X X L N X Q Z O D I U O
O K E C L Y A Y N V Q N C G Q L
U I I K V G R J N G R Q Z D G V
J O V L G S B U R X S S R Q C E
F V R T L S E Q M W N Y O N P R
W M E D E E A A M S O T K E L I
I X R E J E R B L S W X S Z J N
I U L R T K A W P I Y N W J Z E
I Z N U F Q I K H U O N O Y W X
D J O M D U H P Z A W N P G T I
P I T F S W P H C I L R Y P Z F
Q B T P X I V M M N N E Z D A J
```

Oddball Out

In each row, circle the animal that is different from the others.

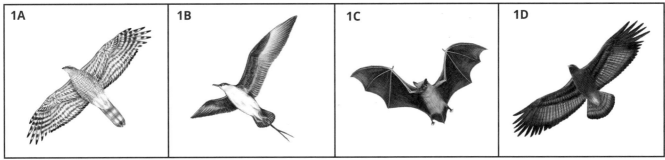

1A 1B 1C 1D

Three of these are birds; one is not.

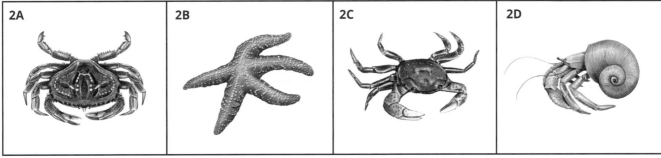

2A 2B 2C 2D

Three of these are crabs; one is not.

3A 3B 3C 3D

Three of these are hoofed mammals; one is not.

4A 4B 4C 4D

Three of these are meat-eaters (carnivores); one is not.

Wildlife Respect

In wild spaces, humans are the visitors. We are lucky to be able to observe animals in their natural habitats. Along with that privilege, comes a responsibility to respect the animals we see, as well as their homes. The best way to learn about wildlife is by quietly watching. Though the possibility of getting a better look – or a better photo – can be tempting, getting too close can be stressful to a wild animal.

Here are some ways you can help reduce the number of disruptive human encounters that wild animals experience:

1. Know the site before you go.

2. When taking photos, do not use a flash, which can disturb animals.

3. Give animals room to move and act naturally.

4. Visit after breakfast and before dinner when wild animals are less active.

5. Do not touch or disturb the animals.

6. Do not feed the animals.

7. Store your food and take your trash with you.

8. Read and respect signs.

9. Do not make quick movements or loud noises.

10. Report any encounters with dangerous animals.